D1364057

Illustrated by
Amy K. Rosenthal

PROJECT

1.

2.

3.

These lists, ideas, and sketches belong to:

_____

PROJECT 1,2,3

1. I will challenge myself to come up with something new every day that can be expressed in a list of 3.
(can be anything: prose, drawings, recipes)

2. I will post it daily at 1:23 pm.

3. I will begin this project on 12/3.

signed,

Amy K.R.

That was the first post of one of my mother's last creative projects. Even when her health was severely declining, Amy Krouse Rosenthal challenged herself to come up with something new every day, because creating is what drove her. She knew that the most fulfilling projects could also be the simplest, so she chose the everyday list— a form that's practical, purposeful, and concise— as her method. During those final weeks I spent with my mom, I watched as she turned ideas percolating in her brain into beautiful art on paper. On day 61 of 123, she had to inform her followers, "There are other things I need to be tending to, creating and focusing on with my limited time."

I hope *Project 1, 2, 3* helps you look at your world through a different lens. You don't need to be as stringent as my mom was in her 1:23 pm deadline. I think you'll find, as Amy did, that there is magic in the number three. It's a Goldilocks measure—neither too little nor too much, but just right. Think about it: The triangle is the strongest and most stable shape, able to redistribute loads of weight better than any other form. We have three primary colors that create an entire rainbow. And who could forget *The Three Musketeers* and *The Three Little Pigs*?

Taking time to appreciate three beautiful moments in your day instead of one can be extremely meaningful. In my mom's famous words, **let's make the most of our time here.**

Paris Rosenthal

POSSIBILITIES for a
FRESH START

1. _____

_____

_____

2. _____

_____

_____

3. _____

_____

_____

_____
date

OPPORTUNITIES
I'd like to PURSUE

1. _____

_____

_____

2. _____

_____

_____

3. _____

_____

_____

_____
date

The

STORY BEHIND
MY NAME

_____

_____

_____

what it means

_____

how it's pronounced

_____

_____

_____

what I love about it

_____

date

THINGS from MY PAST I'LL CARRY INTO the FUTURE

1. _____

_____

_____

2. _____

_____

_____

3. _____

_____

_____

_____
date

PARTS of MY PAST
I WILL FINALLY
SET FREE

1. _____

_____

_____

2. _____

_____

_____

3. _____

_____

_____

_____
date

CREATIVE
CALCULATIONS

_____ × _____ = _____

_____ + _____ = _____

_____ − _____ = _____

(patience + silence) × coffee = poetry

_____
date

A MINI PLAYLIST,
for ME by ME

_____

by _____

_____

by _____

_____

by _____

_____
date

_____

title

1. _____

2. _____

3. _____

_____

date

LINES from an
INSPIRING POEM

"   "
_____

by   _____

_____

_____

_____

_____
date

WHERE I WANT
TO BE when I GROW UP

1. _____

_____

_____

2. _____

_____

_____

3. _____

_____

_____

_____
date

What I'm GRATEFUL for,
PARTICULARLY TODAY

1. _____

2. _____

3. _____

_____
date

TOUGH TOPICS I wish I were better at DISCUSSING

1. _____

_____

_____

2. _____

_____

_____

3. _____

_____

_____

_____
date

CONVERSATIONS I'LL ALWAYS AVOID

1. _____

_____

_____

2. _____

_____

_____

3. _____

_____

_____

_____
date

The
MOST INSPIRING
PEOPLE

1. _____

because _____

_____

2. _____

because _____

_____

3. _____

because _____

_____

_____
date

SOMEONE I should RECONNECT WITH

_____

who?

_____

why?

_____

where?

_____

date

_____

title

1. _____

2. _____

3. _____

_____

date

PLACES that MEAN SO MUCH to ME

1. _____

2. _____

3. _____

_____
date

MOTHER NATURE:

a haiku

_____

5 syllables

_____

7 syllables

_____

5 syllables

_____

date

WORDS that SHOULDN'T EXIST

1. _____

2. _____

3. _____

_____
date

HOW TO DEAL with ANYTHING

1. _____
_____
_____

2. _____
_____
_____

3. _____
_____
_____

_____
date

The
INGREDIENTS of a
GREAT IDEA

_____ tsp / tbsp / cup
_____

ingredient

_____ tsp / tbsp / cup
_____

ingredient

_____ tsp / tbsp / cup
_____

ingredient

_____

date

_____
title

1. _____

2. _____

3. _____

_____
date

THREE PROJECTS
to FINISH (finally!)

1. _____

_____

_____

2. _____

_____

_____

3. _____

_____

_____

_____
date

The OPENING SENTENCES of my MEMOIR

_____

_____

_____

_____

_____

_____

_____

_____

_____

_____
date

SPOILER ALERT!
My MEMOIR'S CLOSING SENTENCES

_____

_____

_____

_____

_____

_____

_____

_____

_____

_____

_____

_____

_____
date

HOW TO BREAK
A BAD HABIT

step 1 _____

_____

_____

step 2 _____

_____

_____

step 3 _____

_____

_____

_____

date

On PUSHING YOURSELF and BEING OPEN to FAILURE

1. _____

_____

_____

2. _____

_____

_____

3. _____

_____

_____

_____
date

TEXCERPTS

(excerpts from books)

1. _____
   _____
   _____

2. _____
   _____
   _____

3. _____
   _____
   _____

---
date

_____

title

1. _____

_____

_____

2. _____

_____

_____

3. _____

_____

_____

_____

date

EXPERIENCES that have TESTED MY TRUE CHARACTER

1. _____

_____

_____

2. _____

_____

_____

3. _____

_____

_____

_____
date

WHEN I SEE _____,
I ALSO SEE _____

1. _____   _____

2. _____   _____

3. _____   _____

a bread tie   the Arc de Triomphe

HOW TO GET
OVER SOMETHING that's
BOTHERING ME

I could _____

_____

_____

I'll definitely try _____

_____

_____

I probably won't _____

_____

_____

_____
date

_____

title

1. _____

_____

2. _____

_____

3. _____

_____

_____

date

HOW TO
PLAY HOOKY

1. _____

_____

_____

2. _____

_____

_____

3. _____

_____

_____

_____
date

THINGS I DO
for MYSELF

1. _____

2. _____

3. _____

_____
date

IMPRESSIONS
I'LL LEAVE on this WORLD

that I was _____

_____

_____

that I always _____

_____

_____

that I never _____

_____

_____

_____
date

QUOTES
to REMEMBER and
RECITE

"

"

by _____

"

"

by _____

"

"

by _____

_____
date

MISSING EMOJI
EXPRESSIONS

◯ = _____

◯ = _____

◯ = _____

💬 ??? = You were texting
something, then stopped.
What were you gonna say?!

_____

date

STATEMENTS
we'd be JUST FINE
WITHOUT

1. _____

_____

2. _____

_____

3. _____

_____

_____
date

WISHES for my
FUTURE SELF

1. _____

_____

_____

2. _____

_____

_____

3. _____

_____

_____

_____
date

QUESTIONS I ASK MYSELF

1. _____ ?

2. _____ ?

3. _____ ?

_____
date

QUESTIONS I'M AFRAID to ASK

1. _____ ?

2. _____ ?

3. _____ ?

_____
date

_____

title

1. _____

2. _____

3. _____

_____

date

MY MOST
HEROIC MOMENTS

1. _____

_____

_____

2. _____

_____

_____

3. _____

_____

_____

_____
date

EXPERIMENTS
that involve **TRUST**

1. _____

_____

2. _____

_____

3. _____

_____

Tell me something you want to be kept
a secret. I will keep the secret forever.

_____
date

WHEN LIFE gives me
LEMONS . . .

1. _____

_____

_____

2. _____

_____

_____

3. _____

_____

_____

_____
date

PEOPLE I DREAM of MEETING and what WE'D TALK ABOUT

1. _____

_____

_____

2. _____

_____

_____

3. _____

_____

_____

_____
date

_____

title

1. _____

_____

_____

2. _____

_____

_____

3. _____

_____

_____

_____

date

The SMELLS of HOME

1. _____

2. _____

3. _____

_____
date

I FEEL YOUNG
AGAIN WHEN . . .

1. _____

_____

_____

2. _____

_____

_____

3. _____

_____

_____

_____
date

HOW TO FIND
your WAY

1. _____

_____

2. _____

_____

3. _____

_____

Pay attention to what you
pay attention to.

HOW TO ACCEPT a COMPLIMENT

1. _____

2. _____

3. _____

_____
date

HOW TO ENDURE
an INSULT with GRACE

1. _____

2. _____

3. _____

_____
date

THINGS that SHOULD LAST FOREVER

1. _____

2. _____

3. _____

_____
date

GREAT ADVICE for MYSELF in FIVE YEARS

1. _____

_____

_____

2. _____

_____

_____

3. _____

_____

_____

_____

date

A.T.M. =

A _____

T _____

M _____

Always Trust Magic

_____
date

#1

#2

#3

HOW TO
PUSH MYSELF:

a rhyming summary

1. _____

_____

2. _____

_____

3. _____

_____

_____
date

FAIRY TALES
that CAME TRUE

1. _____

_____

2. _____

_____

3. _____

_____

_____
date

The EASIEST RECIPE for

_____

step 1 _____

_____

_____

step 2 _____

_____

_____

step 3 _____

_____

_____

_____
date

The Yummiest, Easiest Croutons of All Time

1. Get some cornbread (it's in the bakery section of the grocery store) and cut into cubes.

2. Spread out on a baking sheet and drizzle with olive oil.

3. Bake at 400° for 7-10 minutes until golden brown. Let cool (they will get nice and crunchy) then throw them into salad. Count how many seconds it takes for your guests to say "dang, these are the best croutons ever!"

Amy K.R.

UNEXPECTED USES
for a RUBBER BAND

#1

#2

#3

_____
date

SOME GOOD REASONS to GO AHEAD and DO IT

1. _____

_____

2. _____

_____

3. _____

_____

_____

date

MY MOST
PRESSING THOUGHTS

1. _____

_____

2. _____

_____

3. _____

_____

_____
date

VENN DIAGRAM
of a LOVE/HATE
RELATIONSHIP

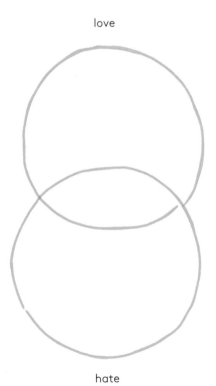

love

hate

_____
date

_____

title

1. _____

2. _____

3. _____

_____

date

I FEEL at ONE with NATURE WHEN . . .

1. _____

_____

_____

2. _____

_____

_____

3. _____

_____

_____

MY LIFE STORY in THREE WORDS

_____

beginning

_____

middle

_____

end

_____

date

HOW TO
FALL IN LOVE

step 1 _____

_____

_____

step 2 _____

_____

_____

step 3 _____

_____

_____

_____
date

When I LOOK OUTSIDE, I SEE . . .

1. _____

_____

2. _____

_____

3. _____

_____

_____

date

DREAMS I REMEMBER

(and don't want to forget)

1. _____

_____

2. _____

_____

3. _____

_____

_____
date

_____
title

1. _____

   _____

2. _____

   _____

3. _____

   _____

_____
date

MOMENTS I'VE SHED TEARS of JOY

1. _____

_____

2. _____

_____

3. _____

_____

_____
date

TIMES I COULDN'T STOP CRYING

1. _____

_____

_____

2. _____

_____

_____

3. _____

_____

_____

_____
date

ME as an
INTROVERT

1. _____

2. _____

3. _____

_____
date

ME as an
EXTROVERT

1. _____

2. _____

3. _____

_____
date

MY WORK, LOVE, AND PLAY:

a pie chart

_____

date

_____

title

1. _____

2. _____

3. _____

_____

date

SUPERPOWERS
I'D LIKE to TRY OUT

1. _____

_____

2. _____

_____

3. _____

_____

_____
date

I GET COMPETITIVE WHEN . . .

1. _____

_____

2. _____

_____

3. _____

_____

_____
date

SYMBOLS that REPRESENT MY VALUES

#1

= _____

#2

= _____

#3

= _____

_____
date

MY THREE BIGGEST
PRIORITIES NOW

1. _____

2. _____

3. _____

_____
date

SMALL THINGS with a BIG IMPACT

1. _____

2. _____

3. _____

_____
date

I'VE SEEN a RAINBOW

_____

here

_____

here

_____

and here

_____

date

_____

title

1. _____

2. _____

3. _____

_____

date

PLACES that BRING OUT the BEST IN ME

1. _____

2. _____

3. _____

_____
date

I CAN'T IMAGINE
a DAY WITHOUT:

a series of sketches

_____

date

WAYS I
BECKON LOVELY

1. _____

_____

_____

2. _____

_____

_____

3. _____

_____

_____

_____
date

TODAY'S RANDOM
ACTS of KINDNESS

1. _____

_____

2. _____

_____

3. _____

_____

_____
date

title

#1

#2

#3

date

EVERYONE
BUT ME is INTO

1. _____

2. _____

3. _____

_____
date

I'M THE ONLY ONE WHO SEEMS to LIKE

1. _____

2. _____

3. _____

_____

date

PEOPLE WHO KNOW
that I LOVE THEM

1. _____

2. _____

3. _____

_____
date

THINGS THAT
MAKE ME, ME

1. _____

_____

_____

2. _____

_____

_____

3. _____

_____

_____

_____
date

NEVER HAVE
I EVER

1. _____

   _____

2. _____

   _____

3. _____

   _____

_____
date

The BEST MESSAGES I RECEIVED this WEEK

date

_____

title

1. _____

2. _____

3. _____

_____

date

WHERE I WAS A YEAR AGO:

a series of sketches

_____

date

MY PERSONAL FAN CLUB INCLUDES

1. _____

2. _____

3. _____

ANYWHERE BUT HERE:

a teleportation itinerary

place	purpose of trip

_____

date

I'VE BEEN DISAPPOINTED WHEN . . .

_____

_____

_____

but _____

_____

_____ ,

and now _____

_____

_____

_____

date

WHEN I CLOSE
my EYES, I SEE . . .

1. _____

_____

2. _____

_____

3. _____

_____

_____
date

_____ in THREE
LANGUAGES

1. _____

2. _____

3. _____

_____
date

STRONG FEELINGS
I'm having **RIGHT NOW**

1. _____

2. _____

3. _____

_____
date

YESTERDAY
COMPARED to TODAY

_____ > _____

_____ < _____

_____ = _____

_____
date

_____

title

_____

_____

_____

_____

date

WAYS OTHERS
would DESCRIBE ME

1. _____

_____

2. _____

_____

3. _____

_____

FUNNY STORIES
from MY CHILDHOOD

1. _____

_____

_____

2. _____

_____

_____

3. _____

_____

_____

_____
date

SKILLS I could TEACH BLINDFOLDED

1. _____

2. _____

3. _____

_____
date

QUESTIONS
I HAVE ABOUT
the WORLD

How _____

_____ ?

When _____

_____ ?

Why _____

_____ ?

_____
date

LET'S BLOW OUT THE
CANDLES TOGETHER!

a wish for _____

a wish for _____

a wish for _____

_____
date

_____

title

1. _____

2. _____

3. _____

_____

date

THINGS to get
OFF MY CHEST

1. _____

_____

2. _____

_____

3. _____

_____

_____
date

HOW TO WRITE
a THANK-YOU NOTE

1. _____

_____

2. _____

_____

3. _____

_____

_____
date

FAVORITE
FAMILY RITUALS

1. _____

_____

2. _____

_____

3. _____

_____

_____
date

TRADITIONS
I WANT to START

1. _____

2. _____

3. _____

_____
date

PEOPLE WHO
ARE LIKE ME

1. _____

2. _____

3. _____

_____
date

PEOPLE WHO
ARE UNLIKE ME

1. _____

2. _____

3. _____

_____
date

HOW TO
SAY NO

step 1 _____

_____

step 2 _____

_____

step 3 _____

_____

_____

date

_____

title

1. _____

_____

2. _____

_____

3. _____

_____

_____

date

WHAT I LOVE ABOUT
the WEATHER (or not)

1. _____

2. _____

3. _____

_____
date

A LETTER I'VE BEEN MEANING to WRITE

(the beginning, middle, and end)

Dear _____,

_____

_____

_____

_____

_____

_____

_____

_____

_____

_____

_____

_____

date

MY GO-TO
DOODLES

#1

#2

#3

_____
date

PERSONAL PALEONTOLOGY:

the evolution of my life

1. age of

2. age of

3. age of

_____

title

1. _____

2. _____

3. _____

_____

date

LESSONS I LEARNED
the HARD WAY

1. _____

_____

2. _____

_____

3. _____

_____

_____
date

LOVE,

three ways

_____

_____

_____

_____
date

HOW HISTORY REPEATS ITSELF

1. _____

_____

2. _____

_____

3. _____

_____

_____

date

ONE PATTERN
I see EVERYWHERE

_____

_____
here

_____
here

_____
and here

_____
date

TIME FLIES
by WHEN . . .

1. _____

2. _____

3. _____

_____
date

TIME SEEMS
to STOP WHEN . . .

1. _____

2. _____

3. _____

_____
date

SNAP, CRACKLE, POP:

a few doodles about sound

_____

title

1. _____

2. _____

3. _____

_____

date

UNFORGETTABLE
PALINDROMES

1. _____

2. _____

3. _____

Was it a rat I saw?

_____

USELESS FACTS I
LEARNED in SCHOOL

(Or, maybe they were helpful?)

1. _____

_____

2. _____

_____

3. _____

_____

_____

_____
date

LINES for my EPITAPH

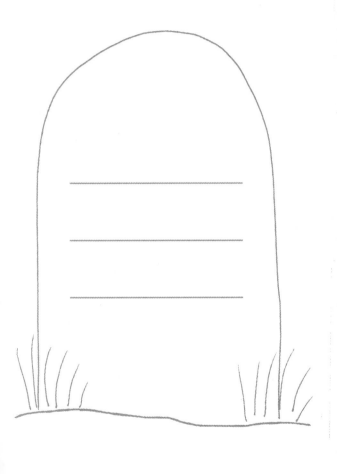

date

I WANT to DIVE RIGHT IN TO . . .

1. _____

2. _____

3. _____

_____
date

LET ME TELL YOU ABOUT the TIME . . .

1. _____

_____

_____

2. _____

_____

_____

3. _____

_____

_____

_____
date

ALL MY LIFE,
I've been WAITING for

1. _____

2. _____

3. _____

_____
date

JOKES I KEEP
in my BACK POCKET

1. _____

_____

_____

2. _____

_____

_____

3. _____

_____

_____

_____
date

GRAMMAR MISTAKES
I've SPOTTED

1. _____

2. _____

3. _____

_____
date

FACTS I
PRIDE MYSELF
on KNOWING

1. _____

   _____

2. _____

   _____

3. _____

   _____

_____

date

TODAY, I'M FEELING . . .

#1

#2

#3

(Answer in anything but words.)

_____
date

HOW TO
BE KIND:

a rhyming summary

1. _____

_____

2. _____

_____

3. _____

_____

_____
date

ANYONE who KNOWS ME UNDERSTANDS

1. _____

_____

2. _____

_____

3. _____

_____

_____
date

And now, it's time to vote for

AMERICA'S NEXT TOP _____

| _____ | _____ | _____ |
| Contestant #1 | Contestant #2 | Contestant #3 |

| _____ | _____ | _____ |

| _____ | _____ | _____ |

| _____ | _____ | _____ |

_____
date

. . . MAMA!

MAMA #1

Has figured out that the question "how was school?" annoys one child but totally engages the other.

MAMA #2

Knows what's going on in the personal life of all current babysitters and past 7 sitters, too.

MAMA #3

When child calls out "Hey, Mom— do you know where that thing with the curly thing is?" this mom knows what she means and where it is!

SHORT ANECDOTES
for the ELEVATOR

1. _____

_____

2. _____

_____

3. _____

_____

_____
date

_____

title

1. _____

   _____

2. _____

   _____

3. _____

   _____

_____

date

When I stare out the window,

I'M MOST LIKELY
THINKING ABOUT . . .

1. _____

2. _____

3. _____

_____

ONE MANTRA,

three times

_____

_____

_____

(Now repeat it throughout the day!)

_____
date

OTHER WAYS to SIGN my NAME

_____

_____

_____

WAYS I KNOW MYSELF really WELL

1. _____

2. _____

3. _____

_____
date

BUCKET LIST
TO-DOS

date

How _____

is a LOT LIKE
an UMBRELLA

1. _____

_____

2. _____

_____

3. _____

_____

_____
title

1. _____

2. _____

3. _____

_____
date

HOW IT FEELS
to have a GOOD CRY

1. _____

_____

2. _____

_____

3. _____

_____

_____
date

GRATITUDE IS AS EASY AS

1. _____

2. _____

3. _____

_____
date

TO FOCUS, I NEED . . .

1. _____

2. _____

3. _____

_____
date

The LAST PEOPLE
I THANKED

_____

_____

_____

_____
date

Ways I feel

EMPOWERED

1. _____

_____

2. _____

_____

3. _____

_____

HOW I REALLY
FEEL TODAY

_____

_____

_____

_____

date

HOW TO
WAKE UP HAPPY:

an experiment

hypothesis

the test

conclusion

_____

_____

title

_____

_____

_____

_____

date

WHEN I FIND A PENNY, I . . .

1. _____

_____

2. _____

_____

3. _____

_____

ROSES of my WEEK

1. _____

2. _____

3. _____

_____
date

THORNS of my WEEK

1. _____

2. _____

3. _____

(Remember to focus on those roses!)

_____
date

ONE BIG,
BLISSFUL EQUATION

+ _____

= _____

_____
date

_____

title

1. _____

2. _____

3. _____

_____

date

HOW TO GIVE
a GOOD HUG

step 1 _____

_____

step 2 _____

_____

step 3 _____

_____

CONSCIOUS CHOICES
I MADE TODAY

1. _____

2. _____

3. _____

_____
date

THREE
AMUSING THINGS

_____

_____

_____

_____
date

TWO TRUTHS
and a LIE

_____

_____

_____

(I'll never tell.)

_____
date

HOW TO
SPEND a HOLIDAY

1.
_____

2. _____

_____

3. _____

_____

_____
date

ROAD TRIPS I
WANT TO TAKE

#1 _____

#2 _____

#3 _____

_____
date

_____

title

1. _____

   _____

2. _____

   _____

3. _____

   _____

_____

date

WAYS TO
BEGIN the DAY

1. _____

_____

2. _____

_____

3. _____

_____

_____
date

HOW TO
RELAX before BED

1. _____

_____

2. _____

_____

3. _____

_____

_____

date

ITEMS I'VE HAD
since CHILDHOOD

1. _____

2. _____

3. _____

_____
date

MEMORIES
I'LL NEVER FORGET

1. _____

_____

2. _____

_____

3. _____

_____

_____
date

LOFTY
ASPIRATIONS

1. _____

2. _____

3. _____

(What are you waiting for?)

_____
date

THREE GOALS
WITHIN REACH

1. _____

2. _____

3. _____

_____
date

LINES
from a LULLABY

---

date

#1

#2

#3

WHAT SOOTHES ME:

a series of sketches

HOW TO DISCOVER
NEW THINGS

1. _____

   _____

2. _____

   _____

3. _____

   _____

_____
date

I BELONG . . .

_____
here

_____
here

_____
and here

_____
date

TEXT CONVERSATION

_____

date

CLEVER ROAD SIGNS

HOW TO MAKE
SOMEONE'S DAY

1. _____

2. _____

3. _____

_____
date

MY CREATIONS

1. _____

2. _____

3. _____

_____
date

_____
title

1. _____

_____

_____

2. _____

_____

_____

3. _____

_____

_____

_____
date

LIFE HACKS

1. _____

_____

2. _____

_____

3. _____

_____

AGE-OLD CUSTOMS
that should NEVER DIE

1. _____

_____

2. _____

_____

3. _____

_____

HOW TO PREPARE
for PUBLIC SPEAKING

step 1 _____

_____

step 2 _____

_____

step 3 _____

_____

_____

_____
date

_____
title

1. _____

2. _____

3. _____

_____
date

THREE WAYS
to get a POINT ACROSS

1. _____

_____

2. _____

_____

3. _____

_____

_____
date

REAL LIFESAVERS

1. _____

_____

2. _____

_____

3. _____

_____

_____
date

STILL LIFE
(color by numbers)

1. _____

2. _____

3. _____

_____
date

WHEN I
LOOK UP at the STARS,
I THINK . . .

1. _____

_____

2. _____

_____

3. _____

_____

_____

date

The MOST TREASURED GIFTS I have RECEIVED

1. _____

from _____

2. _____

from _____

3. _____

from _____

_____
date

COMPARING
my GENERATION to my
PARENTS'

_____ > _____

_____ < _____

_____ = _____

_____
date

_____
title

1. _____

   _____

2. _____

   _____

3. _____

   _____

_____
date

WHAT
we SHOULDN'T
TAKE for GRANTED

1. _____

2. _____

3. _____

_____

date

Things
EVERY HOME
SHOULD HAVE

1. _____

2. _____

3. _____

_____
date

EVERYONE
DESERVES

1. _____

2. _____

3. _____

_____
date

HOW MUSIC MAKES ME FEEL

(Draw your answers.)

#1

#2

#3

_____

date

The DOS and DON'TS of TABLE ETIQUETTE

do this ⟶

← don't do this

do this

_____
date

title

MINDFULNESS,

three ways

1. _____

2. _____

3. _____

_____
date

WHAT I LOOK FOR in a FRIEND

1. _____

_____

2. _____

_____

3. _____

_____

_____

date

TEE-IDEAS

DKNWhy
Bother

HOW TO TRANSFORM A BROKEN HEART:

a series of doodles

#1

#2

#3

_____

date

THINGS I WROTE

1. _____

2. _____

3. _____

_____
date

Love is _____

_____

Love is not _____

_____

Love may be _____

_____

_____
date

UNEXPECTED USES
for a CARDBOARD BOX

#1

#2

#3

_____
date

The MOST ORGANIZED PARTS of MY LIFE RIGHT NOW

1. _____

2. _____

3. _____

_____
date

GAUGING MY FULFILLMENT

empty / full

NATURE

empty / full

BEAUTY

empty / full

ART

_____

date

_____

title

#1

#2

#3

_____

date

THREE FUNNY
THINGS about LIFE

1. _____

_____

2. _____

_____

3. _____

_____

_____
date

WHEN TO APOLOGIZE

1. _____

_____

_____

2. _____

_____

_____

3. _____

_____

_____

_____
date

HOW TO FORGIVE

step 1 _____

_____

_____

step 2 _____

_____

_____

step 3 _____

_____

_____

_____

date

WHAT goes AROUND comes AROUND

1. _____

2. _____

3. _____

_____
date

TINY GEMS

1. _____

_____

2. _____

_____

3. _____

_____

_____

title

#1

#2

#3

_____

date

TRY AS I MIGHT...

1. _____

_____

2. _____

_____

3. _____

_____

_____
date

The _____ ∘∘

ODE to an ORDINARY OBJECT

_____

_____

_____

_____

title

1. _____

2. _____

3. _____

_____

date

ART IS . . .

1. _____

2. _____

3. _____

_____
date

SCHEDULE for a DAY
BY MYSELF

morning

noon

night

_____

date

SOCIAL MEDIA
can be GOOD FOR . . .

1. _____

   _____

2. _____

   _____

3. _____

   _____

_____
date

TRICKS I KEEP
up my SLEEVE

#1

#2

#3

_____
date

CHILDHOOD versus ADULTHOOD

_____ > _____

_____ < _____

_____ = _____

_____

date

_____

title

1. _____

2. _____

3. _____

_____

date

HOW TO LEARN
from a MISTAKE

step 1 _____

_____

_____

step 2 _____

_____

_____

step 3 _____

_____

_____

_____

date

A FEW DETAILS
about my FAMILY TREE

_____
date

ME, after a GREAT PERFORMANCE

#1

#2

#3

WAYS MY LIFE is ORDINARY

1. _____

2. _____

3. _____

_____
date

WAYS MY LIFE is EXTRAORDINARY

1. _____

2. _____

3. _____

_____
date

HOURS of the DAY THAT FEEL like a MINUTE

_____

_____

_____

_____

_____

_____

_____
date

COMPLAINTS that COULD BE POSSIBILITIES

1. _____

_____

_____

2. _____

_____

_____

3. _____

_____

_____

_____
date

_____

title

1. _____

_____

_____

2. _____

_____

_____

3. _____

_____

_____

_____

date

THESE THINGS
BRING VALUE to my LIFE

1. _____

2. _____

3. _____

_____
date

WHEN NOT at HOME, I can be FOUND

_____

here

_____

here

_____

and here

_____

date

ROUTINES
I MAINTAIN

no matter where I am

1. _____

_____

2. _____

_____

3. _____

_____

_____
date

WHEN to TAKE a DEEP BREATH

1. _____

2. _____

3. _____

_____
date

MY MENTORS
for TODAY

1. _____

2. _____

3. _____

_____

date

YAY, MUSIC!

(Turn these staffs into something.)

Music notation is
the one language that
is understood almost
anywhere in the world.

It is the universal gift of G A B

_____

title

1. _____

2. _____

3. _____

_____

date

FRIENDSHIPS:

three conditional statements

If _____ ,

then _____

If _____ ,

then _____

If _____ ,

then _____

_____
date

TERMS OF
ENDEARMENT

_____

_____

_____

_____
date

UNEXPECTED USES
for a TOOTHPICK

#1

#2

#3

_____

date

HOW TO SPEND
A SATURDAY:

a rhyming summary

1. _____

_____

2. _____

_____

3. _____

_____

_____
date

AWARDS for THIS MONTH'S MVPs

☆ _____ ☆

for _____

☆ _____ ☆

for _____

☆ _____ ☆

for _____

_____
date

_____

title

1. _____

_____

2. _____

_____

3. _____

_____

_____

date

In ten years,

I DON'T WANT to FORGET that I . . .

1. _____

_____

_____

2. _____

_____

_____

3. _____

_____

_____

_____
date

GREAT OUTCOMES
from TRUSTING MY GUT

1. _____

_____

_____

2. _____

_____

_____

3. _____

_____

_____

_____

date

MY DAY in SKETCHES

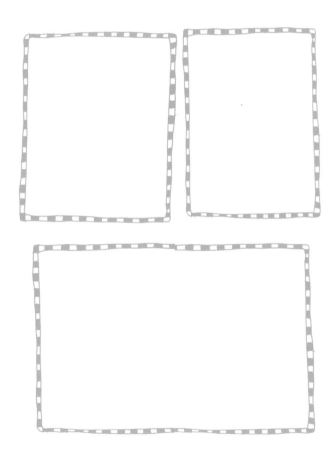

_____
date

EVERY DAY is a
NEW DAY to ENJOY

1. _____

2. _____

3. _____

_____
date

_____

title

#1

#2

#3

_____

date

I COULDN'T
HAVE DONE IT

without the help of

_____ ,

who _____

_____ ,

who _____

and _____ ,

who _____

_____

date

ADULTHOOD, DEFINED

1. _____

_____

_____

2. _____

_____

_____

3. _____

_____

_____

_____
date

The

BEAUTY and OPTIMISM
of a THREE-YEAR-OLD

1. _____

_____

_____

2. _____

_____

_____

3. _____

_____

_____

_____

RAW TALENT, EXPLAINED

1. _____

_____

_____

2. _____

_____

_____

3. _____

_____

_____

_____
date

HOW TO DRAW
INSPIRATION

First you _____

_____

Then you _____

_____

Finally you _____

_____

_____
date

The PROS and CONS of NAÏVETÉ

_____

_____

_____

_____

_____

_____

_____
date

IF I WON
the LOTTERY I'D . . .

1. _____

   _____

   _____

2. _____

   _____

   _____

3. _____

   _____

   _____

   _____
   date

How a **TRUE FRIEND** is a **LOT LIKE** a

1. _____

2. _____

3. _____

The road to the house of a friend is never **long**.

_____
date

_____

title

_____

_____

_____

_____

date

THREE QUICK STEPS
to SLOWING DOWN

1. _____

2. _____

3. _____

_____
date

A RECIPE for SERENI-TEA

_____ tsp / tbsp / cup

_____

ingredient

_____ tsp / tbsp / cup

_____

ingredient

_____ tsp / tbsp / cup

_____

ingredient

_____

date

MY HANDWRITING:

a personal analysis

1. _____

_____

2. _____

_____

3. _____

_____

ABCDEFGHIJKLMNOPQRS TUVWXYZ

_____

date

To me,

PEACE MEANS . . .

1. _____

_____

_____

2. _____

_____

_____

3. _____

_____

_____

_____
date

Pressing pause:
TODAY'S BEST MOMENTS

1. _____

2. _____

3. _____

_____
date

WHAT IF ...

1. _____

2. _____

3. _____

_____
date

MEANINGFUL
CONVERSATIONS

I've had

_____
title

1. _____

   _____

   _____

2. _____

   _____

   _____

3. _____

   _____

   _____

_____
date

MY RELATIONSHIP VALUES

1. _____

_____

2. _____

_____

3. _____

_____

_____
date

I LIKE TO
PONDER . . .

1. _____

_____

_____

2. _____

_____

_____

3. _____

_____

_____

_____

date

HAVE YOU SEEN THIS PERSON?

(descriptions of my best self)

1. _____

_____

_____

2. _____

_____

_____

3. _____

_____

_____

_____
date

THINGS I CROSSED OFF
my TO-DO LIST

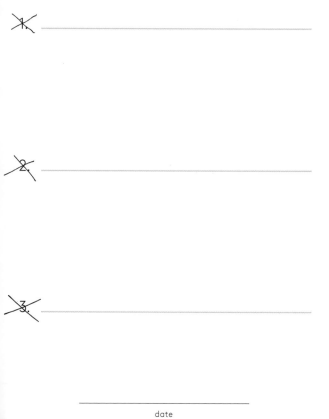

1. _____

2. _____

3. _____

_____
date

CHEEEEESE!

_____ ,

_____ ,

and _____

always put a smile on my face.

_____
date

RIDING the WAVE of RELIEF

#1

#2

#3

_____
date

_____

title

1. _____

2. _____

3. _____

_____

date

BEAUTIFUL
INTERACTIONS

I've witnessed

1. _____

_____

_____

2. _____

_____

_____

3. _____

_____

_____

_____

date

LUCKY
MOMENTS

1. _____

_____

_____

2. _____

_____

_____

3. _____

_____

_____

_____
date

RANKING the month's
BIGGEST VICTORIES

_____

1st

_____

2nd

_____

3rd

_____

date

TIME to STOP and

_____ ,

_____ ,

and _____ .

CIRCLE OF LIFE:

my version of utopia

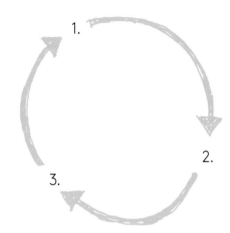

1. _____

2. _____

3. _____

_____

date

#1

#2

#3

WHY the STRUGGLE is WORTH IT

1. _____

_____

2. _____

_____

3. _____

_____

_____
date

OVERCOMING SETBACKS:

a series of doodles

_____

date

MY DREAM
JOB POSTING

Currently seeking _____

_____

Candidate must _____

_____

Responsibilities include _____

_____

_____
date

_____

title

1. _____

2. _____

3. _____

_____

date

Don't mind me:

MY MOST
ENDEARING QUIRKS

1. _____

_____

2. _____

_____

3. _____

_____

_____

date

HOW TO TUNE IN
to an EMOTION

1. _____

   _____

   _____

2. _____

   _____

   _____

3. _____

   _____

   _____

_____
date

WILL TODAY be a GOOD DAY?

a flow chart

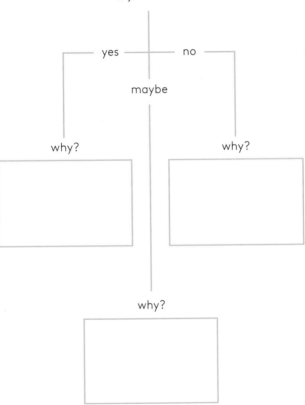

yes — no

maybe

why?

why?

why?

date

WHAT I KNOW
about MY ANCESTRY

1. _____

_____

_____

2. _____

_____

_____

3. _____

_____

_____

_____
date

I COULD
GET USED TO

_____ ,

_____ ,

and _____ .

_____
date

By the end of this month,

I WANT TO HAVE
MADE PROGRESS ON

1. _____

2. _____

3. _____

_____
date

The WORD "COZY"
makes me THINK OF . . .

1. _____

2. _____

3. _____

FUN with ANAGRAMS

(one word arranged three ways)

_____

_____

_____

In a nutshell:

LIFE STORIES of my
FAVORITE PEOPLE

1. _____

_____

_____

2. _____

_____

_____

3. _____

_____

_____

_____

date

Today's

ROLLER COASTER RIDE

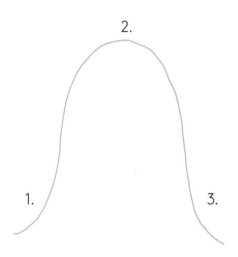

2.

1.

3.

1. _____

2. _____

3. _____

_____
date

My
GOLDEN RULES

1. _____

_____

2. _____

_____

3. _____

_____

_____
date

_____
title

1. _____

2. _____

3. _____

_____
date

HOW TO
TAKE A BREAK

step 1 _____

_____

step 2 _____

_____

step 3 _____

_____

_____
date

MY FAVORITE PEOPLE-WATCHING PLACES

1. _____

2. _____

3. _____

_____
date

LESSONS I'VE LEARNED from OTHERS

1. _____

_____

2. _____

_____

3. _____

_____

_____

date

ITEMS I'D RESCUE from my BURNING HOUSE

(after people and pets)

1. _____

2. _____

3. _____

_____
date

PLACES that HOLD VIBRANT MEMORIES

1. _____

2. _____

3. _____

_____
date

WHY DO
I ALWAYS . . .

1. _____ ?

2. _____ ?

3. _____ ?

_____
date

WHY DO
I RARELY . . .

1. _____ ?

2. _____ ?

3. _____ ?

_____
date

_____
title

#1

#2

#3

_____
date

WHAT I WILL
CHANGE this WEEK

1. _____

_____

2. _____

_____

3. _____

_____

_____
date

THINGS I HAVE LEARNED by DOING

1. _____

_____

_____

2. _____

_____

_____

3. _____

_____

_____

_____
date

HOW TO SPEND
a RAINY DAY

1. _____

_____

_____

2. _____

_____

_____

3. _____

_____

_____

_____

date

MY BERMUDA
TRIANGLE

2.

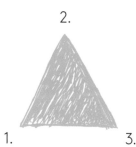

1.   3.

1. _____

2. _____

3. _____

_____
date

A FEW DETAILS about
MY GRANDPARENTS

1. _____

_____

_____

2. _____

_____

_____

3. _____

_____

_____

_____

date

MY DESERT
ISLAND BOOKS

1. _____

by _____

because _____

2. _____

by _____

because _____

3. _____

by _____

because _____

_____
date

_____

title

_____

_____

_____

_____

date

PARTS of my BODY
I APPRECIATE:

a series of doodles

#1

#2

#3

_____
date

EXPERIENCES that have SHAPED MY OUTLOOK on LIFE

1. _____

_____

_____

2. _____

_____

_____

3. _____

_____

_____

_____
date

The

BEST COMPLIMENTS
I'VE RECEIVED

"   "

_____ .

"   "

_____ !

"   "

_____ .

_____
date

A FEW THINGS
that IMPROVE with AGE

1. _____

2. _____

3. _____

_____
date

WHAT INNER BEAUTY
must LOOK like

#1

#2

#3

_____

date

A FEW TWEAKS
to MY DAY that would
MAKE ME HAPPY

1. _____

_____

_____

2. _____

_____

_____

3. _____

_____

_____

_____
date

_____

title

1. _____

_____

2. _____

_____

3. _____

_____

_____

date

That time I CAUGHT a STRANGER'S GAZE

_____

_____

who it was

_____

_____

where it happened

_____

_____

how it made me feel

_____

date

ENCOURAGING WORDS
FOR MYSELF:

a crossword puzzle

1.

2.

3.

A QUESTIONNAIRE

for someone I'm close to

_____
name

1. _____

_____ ?

2. _____

_____ ?

3. _____

_____ ?

_____
date

SHINE ON!

I hope _____ ,

_____ ,

or _____

_____ never fades.

_____
date

NEVER UNDERESTIMATE
THE EXCLAMATION MARK!

1. _____ !

_____

2. _____ !

_____

3. _____ !

_____

_____
date

SOUNDS
of the CITY

1. _____

2. _____

3. _____

_____
date

MY CHILDHOOD BOOKSHELF:

an illustration

_____

date

NEW DEFINITIONS
of *NORMAL*

adjective | nor·mal | 'nór-mal

1. _____

_____

2. _____

_____

3. _____

_____

THINGS I
THINK I NEED

(but wouldn't notice if they disappeared)

1. _____

2. _____

3. _____

_____
date

_____
title

1. _____

2. _____

3. _____

_____
date

REBEL WITHOUT
A CAUSE

(a trip down memory lane)

1. _____

_____

_____

2. _____

_____

_____

3. _____

_____

_____

_____

date

TURN that FROWN UPSIDE DOWN

(Sketch things that make you happy.)

#1

#2

#3

_____
date

COINCIDENCE
or NOT?

1. _____

_____

2. _____

_____

3. _____

_____

_____
date

THE TAO of the
PAPERCLIP

#1

#2

#3

_____
date

HOW TO DRAW
A SMILE

step 1

step 2

step 3

_____

date

I AM ENOUGH

(Let me count the ways.)

#1

#2

#3

_____

date

A TRIO I'D LOVE to GET TOGETHER

#1

#2

#3

I AM HERE:

a self-portrait

1. _____

2. _____

3. _____

_____
date

This is
WHAT DRIVES ME

1. _____

2. _____

3. _____

_____
date

_____

title

1. _____

2. _____

3. _____

_____

date

The LAYERS of MY PERSONALITY

_____
date

JUST WHAT YOU'VE BEEN LONGING FOR

(three short anecdotes)

1. _____

_____

_____

2. _____

_____

_____

3. _____

_____

_____

_____
date

WHERE I
WANT to TRAVEL

_____

city

_____

country

_____

continent

_____

date

THIS WEEK my HEART GOES OUT to

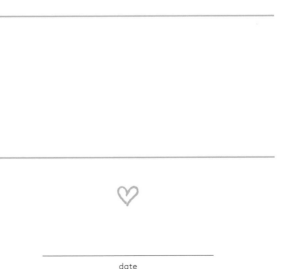

_____
date

An INDEX of MY
FAVORITE THINGS

A _____

B _____

C _____

_____
date

WHAT I
WAS DOING

_____

at 1:23 pm

_____

on 12/3

_____

for 123 minutes

_____

date

I LIKE YOU
I LOVE YOU
I UGH YOU

_____

_____

_____

_____
date

THINGS I CAN
ACCOMPLISH in
THREE SECONDS

1. _____

2. _____

3. _____

I SPY
THREE of a KIND

(things I've seen in threes)

1. _____

2. _____

3. _____

_____
date

title

date

I'VE CHANGED MY MIND ABOUT...

1. _____

2. _____

3. _____

_____
date

NEW LOOKS
for the NUMBER 3

(Finish these sketches.)

A LIST of
MY PRIORITIES

_____

past

_____

present

_____

future

_____
date

FINDING
A BALANCE

not enough

just right

too much

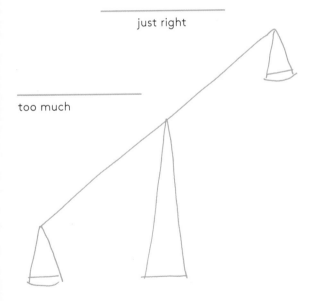

date

A SUMMARY of MY WORK

I came _____

I saw _____

I conquered _____

_____
date

TOP THREE ways to
JUMP-START a GOAL

1. _____

_____

_____

2. _____

_____

_____

3. _____

_____

_____

_____
date

MEMORABLE
MEALS

---

alone

---

with a lover

---

with family

---

date

LAST THOUGHTS for the
END of the YEAR

3. _____

_____

2. _____

_____

1. _____

_____

In the new year
Let's All Shine Together

_____
date

Copyright © 2019 by Paris Rosenthal

All rights reserved.
Published in the United States by Clarkson Potter/
Publishers, an imprint of the Crown Publishing Group,
a division of Penguin Random House LLC, New York.
crownpublishing.com
clarksonpotter.com

CLARKSON POTTER is a trademark and POTTER
with colophon is a registered trademark of Penguin
Random House LLC.

Library of Congress Cataloging-in-Publication Data
Names: Rosenthal, Paris, author.
Title: Project 1, 2, 3 : A daily creativity journal for expressing
yourself in lists of three / Paris Rosenthal.
Other titles: Project one, two, three
Description: New York : Potter, 2019
Identifiers: LCCN 2018017293 | ISBN 9780525575467
(non-traditional format—diary/journal)
Subjects: LCSH: Self-actualization (Psychology) |
Creative ability. | Self-realization.
Classification: LCC BF637.S4 R6747 2019 | DDC 158—dc23
LC record available at https://lccn.loc.gov/2018017293

ISBN 978-0-525-57546-7

Printed in China

Interior illustrations by Amy Krouse Rosenthal
Cover and interior design by Mia Johnson

10 9 8 7 6 5 4 3 2 1

First Edition